Thank You

To my amazing
husband and kids who
tried their best to give
me my me day.

Book title What a Disaster.

Written by Jodie McGregor
Illustrated by Allison Hutchison

First Printing, 2024

Published by Jodie McGregor
jodiestales.com
ISBN 978-0-646-70040-3

What a Disaster

It is very busy at Will and Noah's house. A baby is coming soon, and everyone is busy getting all the jobs done.

Will and Noah make their beds
and tidy their room.

Well, most of the
time. Sometimes they
get distracted.

Dad believes the baby won't notice if areas behind the fridge and under the couch haven't been cleaned in a while, but he understands that it would make Mum happier if they were, so he is happy to help.

After cleaning
and tidying the
boys go to bed
exhausted.

Mum and Dad are so tired they fall
asleep on the couch.

The next morning Mum calls a family meeting.
She thinks it would be a good idea to slow things
down and rest before the baby arrives.
"I think I need a me day."

Dad has decided to take the boys to the farm for the day. They love visiting the farm, especially catching yabbies. However, one thing they don't like is the stinky, snotty cows.

Mum is also planning her day, "I'm going to read my book, grab a coffee, have a piece of my favourite chocolate cake, and finally have a warm, relaxing bath!"

The next morning, Dad and the boys waved bye to
Mum and wish her a relaxing day.

Mum doesn't waste time. She goes down the street to her favourite cafe and orders a cup of coffee and a piece of chocolate cake.

At the cafe Mum runs into an old
friend. So, they both have a chat.
Then, Mum realises the morning is
getting away from her and says to
her friend she has to keep going.

When Mum arrives home, she heads directly to the couch to switch on the TV to watch a movie. However, the TV does not come on. "Oh, that's why," she remembers, the power was scheduled to be turned off this morning.

"Not to worry." she says. Mum decides to have a relaxing bath instead. Mum starts to run the bath then, the doorbell rings.

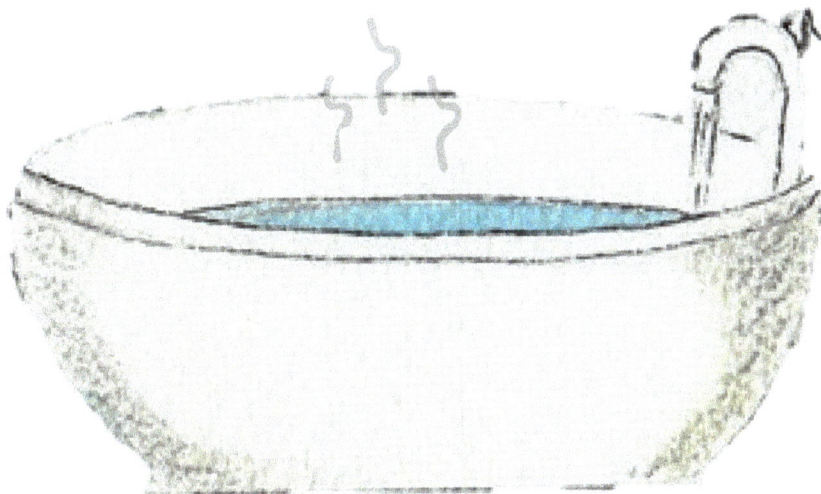

It's the next-door neighbour asking Mum
if she has seen her cat. "No, I haven't but
you're welcome to have a look in the
backyard." says mum.

Mum waits for her neighbour to leave, then begins to run the bath again.

Meanwhile, at the farm, the boys unpack everything. While Dad makes lunch, they cast their yabby nets into the dam.

Uh oh! The cows wander up to where Will and Noah are fishing for yabbies, - "Moo."

Will and Noah get such a fright, they sprint
right into the dam. Even Dad panics, shouting,
"No! Stop!"

Will and Noah get out of the dam, dripping and shivering. "THERE'S SOMETHING CREEPY IN MY BOOT!" Noah screams. Dad rushes to the rescue, "QUICK, DAD! IT'S CREEPING CLOSER, TRYING TO NIBBLE MY TOES!" Noah cries out.

"Noah, you have a.....

"A yabby in your boot!" Dad
says in surprise.

Dad casually flicks the yabby away, and whoosh,
it zooms past William like a speedy rocket!
"Come on, boys," he says. "I reckon it's home
time now."

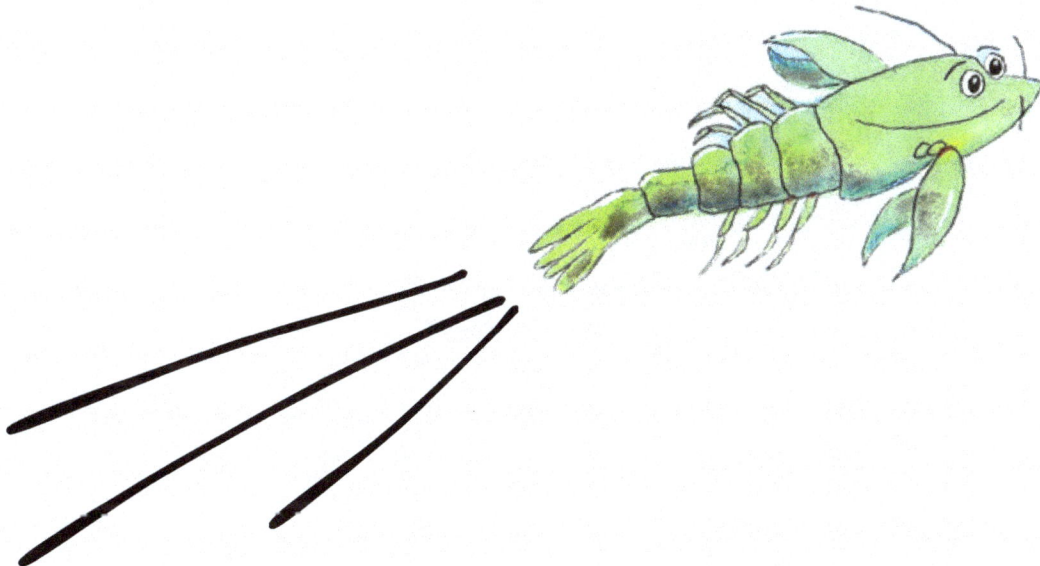

Mum's all set to dive into a relaxing bath when, ring ring! It's Dad. "What a disaster," he says. "How's your day?" he asks. "Not as relaxing as I'd hoped," Mum says. Mum is relieved as she learns everyone's safe and sound, and says she will see them soon.

Mum discovers her bath has turned into a chilly pool while chatting with Dad on the phone. "Oh well," she sighs, as she pulls out the plug and gets dressed.

Mum hears Dad and the boys arrive home. She meets them at the door. "HEY, MUM," Noah yells with excitement. "You won't believe this - I caught a yabby in my boot!" "Well, that's only because you ran into the dam, because you were scared of the cows," teases Will. "Sounds like an interesting story" says Mum.

"How was your 'Me Day', Mum?" Noah asked. "Oh, it turned out to be more of a 'Me Morning'," Mum chuckled. "I had a cup of coffee and indulged in a heavenly slice of chocolate cake." "Is that it?" questioned Will. After sharing a good laugh about their day, Mum spotted the return of power and they agreed to snuggle up on the couch for the remainder of Mum's 'Me Day', watching movies together.

www.ingramcontent.com/pod-product-compliance
Lightning Source LLC
Chambersburg PA
CBHW040252100426
42811CB00011B/1233